MOM
SAID

Published by A Human Foundation Publishing, LLC

Mom Said. ©2004 by Patricia Hogue, Kathy Berger & Patty Soffer
All rights reserved.
Published in the United States by
A Human Foundation Publishing, LLC
http://www.ahumanfoundation.com

Design and composition by Vanessa Flores, sobe-creative.com
ISBN: 978-0-9859173-5-7 (Paperback)
Printed in the United States of America

Youth fades, love droops,
the leaves of friendship fall;
A mother's secret hope
outlives them all.

—Oliver Wendell Holmes Sr.

DEAREST MOM

About ten years ago, Kathy and I were having one of our chats about life and family and stuff. My creative juices were really cookin' in those days. I had just graduated from college at 40 no less and was discovering you CAN teach an old dog new tricks. College had reopened a mind fertile but dulled by years of marriage, divorce and child rearing. Now I wanted MORE! I had these powerful ambitions. I needed to grow. To succeed in a way I knew was expected of me. I HAD to do well because Mom said I was born for great things. Mom said I should be independent. Learn to take care of myself. Use my brain and all else would follow. Mom said I should go out into the world and grab it by the balls.

I always did what Mom said. We all did. Mom's words were gospel to us, and in them we found safety, guidance, reprimand, cheerleading, humor and sass. Most of all, we found love. She just has a way. It's hard to explain, but the best I can do is to say she plays on the black keys only.

So Kathy and I decided it was high time we harnessed what Mom said for posterity. And in doing so, we realized the whole family, from Great Grandpa Tracy on down, has a way with words that's something to behold. It's truly a gift.

And now, Mom, here's our gift to you. We hope you enjoy *Mom Said*. Your poems and recipes, family stories and photos remind us all of the great and powerful life we have been privileged to share. And it's a privilege being your daughter.

Mom Said comes from your heart. All we did was put it together. It's quite a legacy and you should be very proud of a life well spent. Just look around you. This is the best gift of all.

I love you, Mom. Happy 75th Birthday!

Patty

Note that "gas" seems to be a common theme over the next few pages and you've passed that down to us as well (pun intended!).

ON YOUR 75ᵀᴴ BIRTHDAY
SEPTEMBER 6, 2004

This project started out simply as a gift for you. What I have discovered is that it is one of the best gifts I have ever given myself. And it is a gift I will now give to my children and to my grandchild who is on the way.

Reconnecting with the past has been many things. Emotional. Heartwarming. Cathartic. And even a little surprising. But most of all, it is a peek backwards into the way you were loved as a young girl, and into the ways you gave so much love over the years to your family and friends.

I didn't learn to cook nearly as well as you, I could never bleach a load of laundry the way you can, and I certainly won't ever play piano or write poetry like you do. But if I can love my family with the same warmth and caring that you show us all, I will have learned the best lesson in life.

With incredible love and gratitude,
Your daughter,

Kathy
Kathy

1955

1997

THE
EARLY
YEARS

FAMILY POEMS FROM THE PRAIRIE

On last Friday, by the postman
    Came a letter to our wigwam.
Came a writing full of good cheer
    From the land of Pennsylvania,
From the land of stone and hardpan
    From the land of stumps and briers.

Very glad we were to get it
    Glad to hear from friends of afar off,
And we wish we might hear oftener
    Oftener might receive your letters
But very for those you do send
    And to answer I'll endeavor

I will tell you what we're doing
    How we live and how we labor
That the tribes of men may prosper
    Eating bread and cakes next winter,
Made from wheat well raised last summer.
    In the same song I will tell it
That you used when writing to us.

In the first place I will tell you
    What each weekday brings unto us,
In the morning when the timepiece
    To the hour of three is pointing,
Seems to murmur,"Oh! my Children--
    Day is long the nights mere nothing.
Get you up and feed your horses."
With regrets we leave our slumbers
Forth unto the farm we wander,
    Fly around and tend the horses
Harness them and clean the dirt off.

When our breakfast we have eaten
    Out we go unto the prairie,
Where no plow e'er turned a furrow
    Where the bison used to wander,
Even now we trace their footpathes
    Here and there across the prairie.
And the ground is scattered over
    With the bones of this old monster,
And they bother us the worst kind
    Sometimes make us feel like swearing
Dull our plows to beat the dickens.

Sixteen miles each day we travel
    With our team and plow before us,
And the plows we have to sharpen
    Two or three times every half hour.
Hal and I, we do the farm-work,
    Father mostly works at odd jobs.
Built a house and dug a cellar.
    Jumped a claim and put a house on.
Nicest land you ever heard of.
    Distance from the railroad, four miles.
Once each week he sleeps all night there,
    This in order to retain it.

Well, I've told you how we prosper,
    What we do and how we do it;
I will speak now of the country
    Of its likes and of its dislikes,
Anything that I may think of,
    That will lengthen-out my letter.

Though we have no stones or hardpan,
    Though we have no stumps and briers;
Though we have no building fences
    Still it is not all smooth sailing.
We have many things against us,
    From June the first 'til late October
All is well there's nothing nicer.
    All the fault that I can find is
With the troublesome mosquito.
    But the winters are quite tedious,
And the springs, they are a caution;
    Cold and wet and fearful muddy.

And this is not all the drawbacks.
    If you have no building fences,
You've no gate to swing upon.
    Even if you found a gate here
There's no girl to swing it with you.
    Should you find both girl and gate-post
Still you could not swing thereon
    For mosquitoes are so thick,
They'd eat you, if you swing long.
    Well I think I've said enought now
'Bout the land and of the climate
    In the land of the Dakotas,
In the land where are no women.

All the folks are well as usual,
    All except your humble servant.
He's been troubled with the toothache,
    Ached like sixty, ached the wholetime,
Morning, noon, night and midnight.
    Fifty miles I had to journey,
Just to get the blamed old thing out
    But 'twill ache again no more now,
All is peacefull in that quarter.

I'll stop this, this is enough now,
    I'll write again some day I trow,
And let you know the why and how
    Of our Dakota farming.
And if you have a little time
    Just sit you down and write a line
And tell us how you pass your time.
    You might do it when it's storming.

Give my love to all the friends
    Have them write if they have pens,
If not borrow other mens
    And greet us through a letter.

                    Written by- G. W. Tracy

Grandpa & Grandma Tracy
and family, circa 1930s

GROWING UP IN
POLLOCK
SOUTH DAKOTA

There was fun and laughter,
In our house the other day.
The Mathewson's came trudging up
And cribbage we did play.

They doffed their hats and over-shoes
And gathered round the table.
Rae looked like Lou Costello
And Edward like Clark Gable.

The cards were shuffled and mixed up
Each one drew from the pack.
The lowest number won the deal
And behold it was a Jack.

Winnie was my partner,
And started out with five.
Rae put on a secondone
And I made a nose-dive.

The count was fifteen-two for eight
Oh for another five.
Ed had it and he played it.
Man oh man alive.

Twelve they made upon that play,
The game had just begun.
Winnie played a face-card
And Rae made thirty-one.

The hours flew by, the game went on,
The cards were dealt again,
Some-times our faces shone with joy,
Again a look of pain.

We were, ahead, we won the game,
Our hearts with pride did swell.
While all around the table
There was an awful smell.

We should have been so happy
Knowing we had won the bout.
But there was no joy in our house,
Mighty Edward had passed out.

Poem by Anna Knudson

e.   Whi.
    ghter   Upon
        er day.   I met   stance
            came trudging up   His to   was low and beat.
        se we did play.

They doffed their hats and over-shoes   I hardly knew this friend of mine
And gathered round the table   We were school-mates at twenty,
Rae looked like Lou Costello   He'd changed into an old, old man
And Edward like Clark.   Resembling B.O.Plenty.

The cards were shuffled, and mixed up,   His hair was long, his eyes were dim,
Each one drew from the pack.   The wrinkles they did show.
The lowest number won the deal.   His beard, I never saw the like,
And behold it was a jack.   T'was four inches long I know

Winnie was my partner   His shoulders stooped, his gate was slow,
And started out with five.   He tottered when he walked.
Rae put on a second one   His toothless mouth flew open wide
And I made a nose-dive.   He stuttered when he talked.

The count was Fifteen-two for eight   I asked him how he fared this year
Oh for another five.   He said "Oh not so good,
Ed had it and he played it   my frau lives in the city,
                                         And I out in the woods".

Twelve they made upon that play   I'm tired of living all alone,
The game had just begun   I fear I'm going mad.
Winnie played a face-card,   For she's staying with her mother
And Rae made thirty-one.   And all she does is gad.

The hours flew by, the game went on   "One week at home, the other three
The cards were dealt again.   She's spending in the city.
Some-times our faces shone with joy   While I at home am slinging hash
Again a look of pain.   To chickens, dogs and kitties.

We were ahead, we won the game   Good bye my friend, he said to me
Our hearts with pride did swell   Although my feet have blisters
While all around the table,   I'm walking out to Jonesville
There was an awful smell.   And shaving off these whiskers"

We should have been so happy   He smiled at   that,
knowing we had won the game   And   is hard to beat.
but there was no joy in our house   This was The discription of Jim Jones
    End   then he grew whiskers for the Golden J
                                         ubilee at Bismarck last year.   PA7

Your parents
Ed & Anna Knudson
circa 1940s

11

CARDS
GAMES &
ROOMERS

Ed and Anna were the original "bed and breakfast" hosts. Their rooming house was filled with train men and others who were just passing through. From fresh donuts in the morning to cards and canasta at night, the Knudson rooming house was home to all.

CANASTA

I love to play canasta, it thrills me through and through
To sit across from Neimann and meld a deuce or two.

And maybe in a foursome, have Howard as my mate,
Lay down the wrong, hold up the right, and see his look of hate.

I love to play with Jeannie, too, she's nearly always able
To lay her cards down, all at once, a canasta on the table.

Donnie plays for all he's worth, a' calling for the bug (joker)
And watching out for penalties with a smile upon his mug.

But, best of all, I love to play with Winnie on my side,
Against Ed and Rae, our husbands, as toward the goal we glide.

The games we played not long ago were really nothing slow,
The deuces, treys, and aces were dealt to us, you know.

Ed held a joker and four kings, a deuce and several jacks,
While Rae held only low cards, Ed yelled, "Play, Rae, you sap!"

Without a deuce he couldn't play, the minimum was plenty,
The discard pile he couldn't take to meld one hundred twenty.

I drew a card and laid it down, to Ed 'twas bitter gall,
Winnie played a "stop" card and Raymond started to bawl!

I drew another from the pack while Edward sat there frownin'
At kings and deuces in his hand, but still he wouldn't down 'em.

'Twas Winnie's turn to play again, she made a real canasta,
The looks they gave her seemed to say, "If we could only blast ya!"

Poor Rae sat there a' sweating, his face a' growing redder,
While Edward gave him orders to "draw a card and spread 'er."

My turn again, I drew a card, it matched the ones I held,
With tens and deuces in my hand I made another meld.

We won three out of four that night, our nerves were really fluttered,
You should've seen their faces and heard the things they muttered!

Ed said, "Canasta's not my game, I shouldn't play at all."
And Raymond, too, agreed with him, for them 'twas their downfall.

To have their wives defeat them was quite humiliating,
And I doubt we'll ever play them at another family dating.

COMMENTS
Rae: "It's all right, but I want you to know that I didn't bawl!"
Ed: "Well, I was sure mad, and I wouldn't lay 'em down."
Howard: "I always get mad and say something I'm sorry for."
Neimann: "Don't let 'em get that pile."
Donnie: "I was sure looking for that bug."
Winnie: "I'm sure glad we won."
Jean: "Well, I'm not ready to go out YET."
Anna: "I hope they don't get mad at me."

Anna Knudson - circa 1940s

OUR TRIP OUT WEST

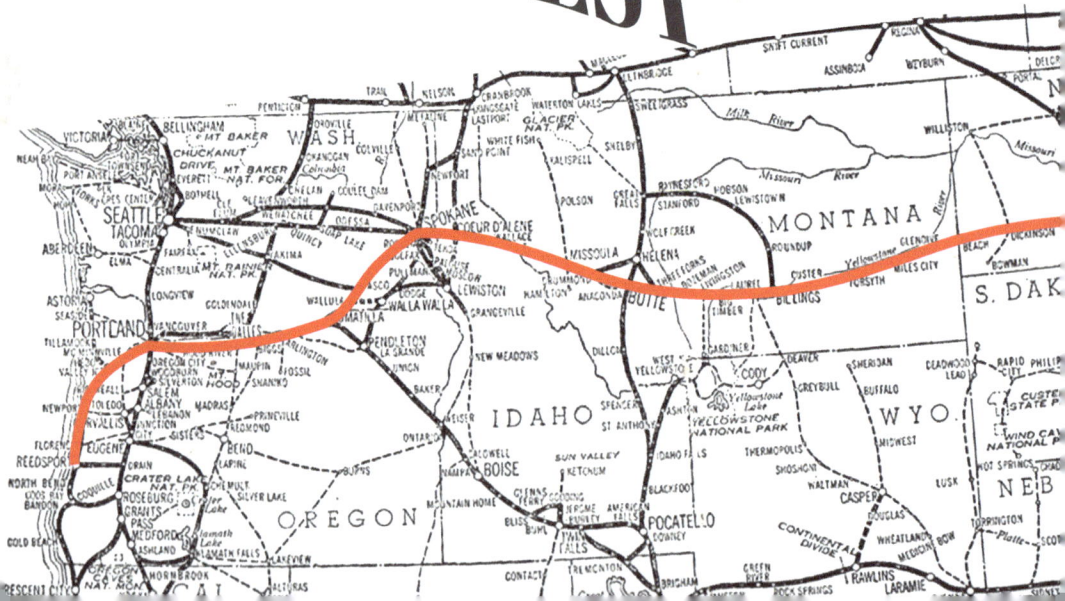

OUR TRIP OUT WEST

'Twas the nineteenth of December when we started on our trip
   Out ___ to See the Olsons and our little grandson, "Chip," (Craig Robert)
Ray ___ ___ took us across the South Dakota line,
   Into the town of Bismarck just about noontime.
We ate dinner with the Worres, with Flo and Aaron Brett,
   Had turkey and all its trimmings, I'll say 'twas nothing flat.
We called ___ ___ Fird, and Art, also Bird and Thor,
   At five we left the Koenigs to lunch with the DeBoers.
We had a ___ ___ meal, from cocktails to ice cream,
   Served in the cutest dining room I think I've ever seen.
We flew from there next morning on the Northwest Air Lines,
   Met Pat in the town of Billings, also some friends of mine,
We saw Aunt Mabel and Kenney, a truly wonderful pair,
   Also Pete and Margaret, they asked us their car to share.
They drove us all over Billings--Ed ward, Patricia, and me--
   It was decorated for Christmas, a magnificent sight to see.
We flew to Portland that evening, 'twas a wonderful trip for me,
   And I'll take my chances anytime in the sky than out on the sea.
We flew over cities, rivers, and hills, between mountains crowned with snow,
   Over Spokane, the beautiful city, and the aluminium plant below.
We reached the city of Portland and landed about 2 A.M.
   Ate lunch at "Jolly Joan's Cafe", had coffee, eggs, and ham.
We stayed all night with the Hagens--Paul and Opal, a jolly pair,
   Then on to Reinhold Peterson's, their dinner with them to share.
We met their daughter, Edith, her children and husband, Tom,
   Also William, his brother, a banker from our home town.
We saw Allen Dyer's sister, Kate, a good position she hold,
   In the largest store in Portland, and leaving money. I'm told,
We rode up in the elevator to the top of ___ ___ ___ ___
   ___ ___ on the escalator to many floors below.
We went to the United Artists and there saw "Adam's Rib."
   Starring Hepburn and Tracy, such wonderful acting they did.
Then down to the "Little Bohemian Cafe"--we had chicken a la king
   Served with ___ rolls, and coffee, a real napkin, too, by jing!
We saw the mighty Pacific with the breakers rolling high,
   The sand dunes and the mountains that stretched up toward the sky.
The Greyhound followed the ocean for a hundred miles or two,
   And riding so close beside it, we three more nervous grew.
A beautiful sight is the Spouting Horn, that, too, is by the oceanside,
   The driver stops to view it as tho it were his pet pride.
We were in the cave by the ocean where the sea lions come and go,
   Lying on rocks and ledges, fighting and growling so.
We also saw the King of the Rock, surrounded by his harem,
   We had to speak in whispers for fear that we would scare 'em.
The Goddess of Liberty we saw, outlined on the walls of it ebore,
   And the face of Abraham Lincoln, as tho it were chiseled in stone.
Then out of the cave and on our way through bridges and tunnels so old,
   Through forests so deep that the sun never shines, and the trees are
                           covered with mold.
'Twas a beautiful drive and we'll never forget just how our stomachs churned,
   When we turned the curves and met the cars and oh, for home we yearned.
We walked out on the sand bar and watched the waves roll by,
   We gathered shells and fossils, so pretty to the eye.
We were down on the wharf of Winchester Bay and viewed the ships afar,
   So many fishing vessels just this side of the bar.
On the other side is the ocean, you could hear its mighty roar,
   Like the boom of a thousand cannon as we stood upon the shore.
We crossed the Umpqua River with its' drawbridge looming high,
   And the big ships going through it was a glorious sight to ___ ___.
We went on a drive to Scotsburg and rounded Dead Man's Curve,
   And I'll swear we were going sixty, the way that car did swerve!!
We finally reached the Olson home at the foot of Gardiner Mountain,
   A cute little cottage surrounded by trees and a bay with lots of trout-in.
We saw our little grandson, "Chip", a beautiful, healthy lad
   With the proudest, happiest parents that a baby ever had.
We stayed two weeks with our children--Edward, Patricia, and me--
   Then Darby came from Southern Cal, drove in on Christmas Eve.
We were such a jolly family as we gathered around the tree,
   And we prayed for those not with us that they might as happy be.
We met their friends, the Duffins, the Abbotts and Durbins we saw,
   Del, Terry, and Harry Rose, the Nelsons (Harry's in-laws.)
Now, just a word before I close, about the Olsons proper,
   I'll tell you what they're doing, how they live and prosper.
Ruth's a busy housewife and works from early morn,
   Taking care of little "Chip" and cooking for her Norm.
Norm's a coach in Reedsport High and really going strong,
   We're only ___ one ___ me, so far, no matter whom they've done.
Patricia's in Montana, in her second year of college,
   She's living in Great Falls, and attends the School of Knowledge.
Our visit soon was ended and again back on the plane,
   We flew above the mountains, above the fog and rain.
Back to the city of Bismarck amid the ice and snow,
   And I know when we reached Pollock it was twenty-five below!
We loved our trip to the western coast, we were thrilled with the ride on
                             the plane,
   But give us good old Pollock, it's nice to be home again.

Patsy Knudson - 1946

PATSY'S
FIRST
CRUSH

He Proposed,
But Dad Won!

In all the seventeen years of my life,
I've written many a poem.
But none about the handsome guy
Who's a paying guest at our home.

He's a brakeman on the S oo Line,
A really wonderful guy.
But oh! He has one single fault!
And that is being shy.

He never tries to flirt with me
The reason I can't see,
I didn't think that there was anything
Radically wrong with me.

Occasionally he asks me for a dance,
But still I'm just a friend.
He just can't see a great romance
With me on the receiving end.

He used to go with Mary,
She's not goodlooking, either,
She must have had a fatal charm,
A nd me, well, I've got neither.

I don't see how she got him,
She must have used a trap,
I've tried almost everything
But falling in his lap!

He probably knows I like him
And treats it like a joke,
'Cuz why else would he treat me
Like a case of poison oak?

The age-old adage about the way
To a mans heart may be true right,
But all I've ever noticed is that
It just increases his flight.

I've tried making cookies,
And graham cracker pies,
But still I've seen no tender light
Shining in his eyes.

As a last resort, I tried perfume.
Black magic, Tabu and Surrender,
But it never took effect and made
Him say things that were tender.

Other people know about
My hopeless infatuation,
A nd they've joined in and tried to help,
My friends and my relation.

Dear Aunt Winnie and Uncle Ray
Have tried to do their best
Ray lays the groundwork while at work
And I'm to do the rest!

But it's so darn hard to try to attract
A so shy and elusive a man.
But I intend to do my best and
Catch him if I can.

There's been a lot of other guys
My interest they've tried to revive,
But instead, I sit at home and wait
For the Pelleck Soo to arrive.

And when it does, it's so awfully late
I never get a chance,
He seems to think a good nights sleep
Must come before romance.

I guess I'm just unlucky
A nd born four years too late,
(Another reason why I just
Can't seem to get a date.)

But maybe he will see the light
And see I'm not too bad,
If he comes to that conclusion
I'll be ready to be had.

But until then I guess I just
Must try to resign myself,
And therefore must forever lay
My affections on the shelf.

Before I close I'd like to say
A few things if I'm able,
About the way my fellow looks
My Johnson, Lawford and Grable.

He's six foot one, has eyes of brown
And dark brown curly hair,
His smile is cute and on top of that
He dances like Fred Astaire.

Aside from that, I could mention
Other things that I've found true,
About the guy I'm crazy 'bout
But I might be boring you.

The way he ignores me you'd think I was
Gravel Gerty and B. O. Plenty,
I'd really go to town on him
If I were only twenty!

And so we'll leave this guy who
Makes my heart beat like a hammer,
And if you still don't know his name
I'll tell you, it's Darby Kramer.

OFF TO

COLLEGE

Mom Attends
Northern State Teachers College
in Aberdeen, South Dakota

It was early in September,
On a morning bright and clear,
That our darling Patsy left us,
Off for a college career.

She was just a small town Lassie,
Blond, slim and tall,
A friend of everybody's,
We loved her one and all.

The house was grim and silent,
No laughter or noise,
Just we two old people,
Surrounded by her toys.

We miss the call of Mom and Dad,
The way she romped with Tim.
The echo has long since died,
Our eyes with tears are dim.

We miss the books and papers,
All scattered round the floor,
The peanut shells and candy,
And Gum wrappers galore.

To night our home will joyful be,
Our girl is coming home.
Enough of college life she's had.
No more she wants to roam.

nna Knudson - 1945

19

Ed and Anna Knudson   Pat and Buster Hogue   Kathryn Ryan Hogue
July 15, 1950

I
—
D O

ODE TO DEAR OLE DAD
ON HIS 70TH BIRTHDAY

THE STORY OF OUR FAMILY

I m here to write a poem about my husband and our Dad.
He s just about the greatest one a family ever had.
He came into this world of ours in 1923
The cutest little fellow that you would ever see.

A family friend, Bill Olson, saw the newborn right away.
He said, I ve got a better name for him than Rolly Ray.
He promptly called him Buster, and that name has really stuck.
He s tried real hard to change it, but he s never had good luck.

His dad a pioneer doctor, mom Kathryn was a nurse.
That same year Doc built the hotel, in fact, that happened
first.
He grew up tall and handsome, but when he was just eleven
His dad died from infection and, we trust, moved on to heaven.

Kathryn then had quite a job
The hotel and her son.
It wasn t easy as those days
Were hard for everyone.

At age fifteen, he went away to school at Notre Dame.
Pretty young for leaving home, but he was brave and game.
He jumped right into track and field and gave it all he had
Enjoyed the track meets and trips, this North Dakota lad.

World Was II began, he joined V-12 at college.
Gave Uncle Sam a chance to pay the balance of his knowledge.
Princeton, N. Y. Columbia, Ann Arbor he was sent
The Navy s youngest ensign, and off to war he went.

Thank God he never got a chance
To fight and be a hero.
The war was almost over
And his battle scars were zero.

Back to North Dakota and to school at N. S. U.
Home again to Linton not quite sure what he would do.
Linton, south of Bismarck, where Beaver Creek runs through
If you don t find that humorous, how s Seeman Park to you?

Little Buster

The Willows Hotel in Linton, ND

Lieutenant Buster at Notre Dame

He took up golf and got quite good, played more than he really should.
He loved to hunt and one fall day, he wandered down to hunt my way.
Twas in the fall of 48, me a teacher, this was fate.
While walking home from school one day, a car drove by, a voice said hey!

He slowed the car and drove aside, and said
 Jump in and have a ride. With him, my friend
from college days, but Buster was who caught
my gaze. So good looking, really neat, I felt my heart
begin to beat. We spoke a while as people might,
he asked May I come back tonight?

This is how my husband, Buster, came into my life.
He immediately warned me I m not looking for a wife.
 I quite agree, I said. At least that s what I made him think.
But deep inside, I knew I d lead this critter to drink.

And so began our life as two. I felt like I d been born anew.
It took two years to tie the knot. July 15th - gosh, it was hot!
Linton was our home to be. We started on our family tree.
T wasn t long, I don t mean maybe, we found we were to have a baby.

Ten months later, to the day, we welcomed little Rollie Ray.
And not much time before we knew, another little one was due.
Kathy joined us, what a joy, a perfect family, girl and boy.
But dear friends, little did we know. We d soon be joined by Patty Jo.

And when we thought there d be no more, Michael evened up the score.
The perfect family, two of each. Teri put that out of reach.
Mary joined the Rhythm Band. Really, this was out of hand!
Birth control came on the scene or we d have numbered seventeen.

Those were all the glory years.
Love and laughter and some tears.
Handsome kids and all so bright. We thanked the good Lord every night.
To be so blessed in every way, and have it still be so today.

Love at the Pump Room in Chicago

So soon they left the Hogue abode and started down life s bumpy
road.
It makes us happy now to say, they re still the greatest kids today.
Tina, Tony, Carl and Lee (some fell off the family tree!)
To tell you how our family grew, we ve grown from two to twenty-
two.

To name them all would take some time
To try and make this damn poem rhyme.
Mike and Jay are Kath & Lee s.
Bear with my meter, if you please.

Marco is Tony and Mary Lynn s,
this is where the fun begins.
Tina and Mike, Chris, Kate and Maddie.
Alex and Sam belong to Patty.
Christy and Doug, Annette and Rollie s,
I m stuck to rhyme that one, by golly.

Now we re in our golden days.
They still show love so many ways.
Phone calls, letters, visits too.
End each one with I love you.
Because these kids are all so great
We meet tonight to celebrate.

So Happy Birthday, Buster dear.
From all of us, both far and near.
Lets do it all again
How about next year???

Patty & Kathy, 1957

Kathy, Rollie, Mike and Patty
Christmas, 1958

Mom and Patty, 1955

Rollie, Kathy, Patty, Mike, Teri, Mary, 1963

SILLY

SWEET

FAMILY

STORIES

Chris Singer, Tina and Mike Hogue

Lee, Kathy, Michael and Jay Berger

Carl, Tiana and Teri Ciarfalio

Kate, Mike and Maddie Hogue

Doug and Christy Hogue

Samantha Fields, Patty Soffer, Alex Fields

Hogue Family Reunion, 1998

Marco and Mary Caldarone

On Having
Too Many Kids

My mother opened up her mouth
Whatever are you doing?
I said I think that my response is
We enjoy the screwing!

Before long Michael joined us
Our relatives kept score.
Any whenever they were near us,
They'd say "how many more?"

Teri was five and Mary six
There must be something the doc can fix.
And so the results of all this play
I'll celebrate on Mother's Day.

We Forgot your Anniversary
No one but us To Blame!
We Note's Lapse in
memory
Lets see_"what is
your name"?

Artwork by Pat Hogue

My eyelids need lifting
My chin is now double
I'm nearing age 70
And that sure means trouble.
My boobs are still firm
That's really the shits.
I should cover my face
And then bare my tits.

My fifty-year marriage to Buster
Took all the grit that I could muster.
If he doesn't improve, we'll still make the move
Me to Rapid and he off to Custer.

I'm 43 and everything sags.
My butts a mess, and my eyes have bags.
But the things that time does change
A plastic surgeon can rearrange.

While sitting in my living room
I thought I heard a sonic boom.
I checked the walls, the window glass,
That sound came out of Buster's ass.

There once was a girl, Paula J.
Bill asked for a blow job, they say.
It certainly shows that her long,
crooked nose
Would definitely get in the way.

Bill Clinton is one handsome fellow
And rumor says, great in the sack.
Kennedy had many women
Not much of a lover-he had a bad back.
Lyndon was not very handsome
But horny as one of his bulls.
And Reagan was much too forgetful.
He may have forgot where it goes.
I must not forget our George Bush
With a wife who looked more like his mother.
I'm sure he was like all the others
But managed to keep under cover.

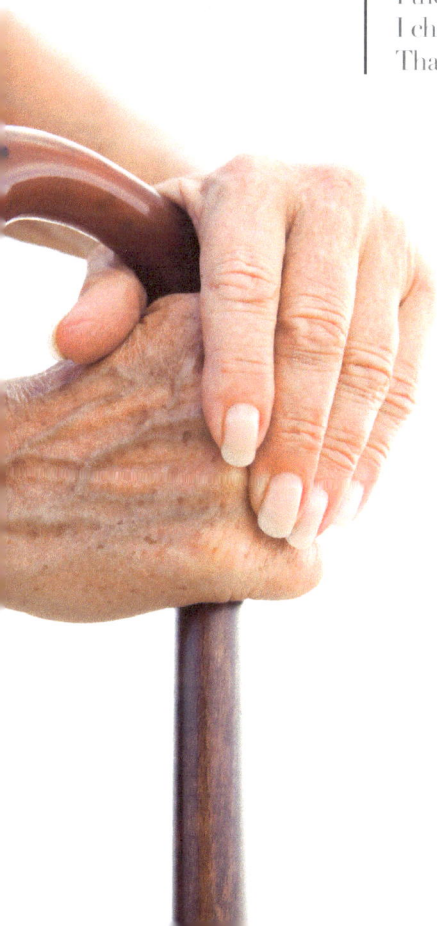

BIRTHDAYS
MOM'S
WAY

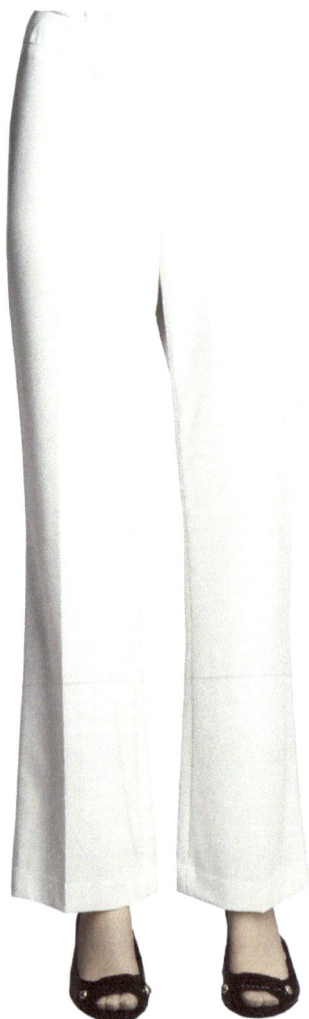

Poem for Pat Tracy on his 70th Birthday

I wish we were there with you tonight
To see you basking in the light
Of friends and family who toast your day
We'll do the same, though far away.

To celebrate your 70 years
Enjoy yourself with several beers.
The years have flown, we're aging fast
Our youth long gone, how quickly passed.

Not the lover you used to be?
Now it's mostly used to pee.
Early to bed, the same to rise
Then coffee with the other old guys.

A peek at the paper to check the obits
Thank God, our names aren't listed in it!
Eat a lot, but knowing that
We pay with extra body fat.

Baseball, basketball, and all that sort
It's out - and chess is the safest sport.
Golf's okay but if you're smart
You'll buy an electric golfing cart.

And yet, it's great to be alive.
So, live another twenty-five.
You're a very lucky man to "getta"
Darling girl like wife your Loretta.

But, Pat, it almost breaks my heart
To know we're just a year apart!

To Myself

Oh, dear, I've lost my family tree.
And I'm not sure how old "I be."
I've never liked a birthday bash
No gifts, although I don't mind cash!

When someone asks me, "What's your age?"
I answer them quite swiftly.
I'm sorry I don't really know
Truth is, I'm only fifty.

So please don't give me birthday blessing
Or here's one gal that you'll be missing.
I'll pack my bag and go someplace
Where no one there gets on my case.

Where someone's birthday's no big deal
You're just as old as how you feel
A word of advice from me that's useful
Don't wear white slacks when on Metamucil.

On Being 50

Fifty isn't really old
A nice round number, I've been told.

Fifty Kisses can't be beat
Fifty Hershey's - really sweet
Fifty Smiles makes your heart boom
Fifty Farts can clear the room
Fifty Years will swell your eyes
Fifty Apples make 8 pies

Nothing wrong with Fifty Bucks
But turning 50 really sucks!

ORIGINALLY
WRITTEN FOR
BART SLEPIAN

GOD REST HIS
SOUL!

Bart my dear, what's this I hear?
You've reached that epic 50th year?
It's not so great to be 2 and 1/2 score
(We women mind it so much more!)

You start to look for old age signs
The nose enlarges and oh those lines.
The waistline grows, the buttocks shrivel
And when you eat, you often dribble.

A hint of heavy, ugly jowls
And things you can't escape from
A worry over aging bowels
With a bit of constipation.

Be careful when you sneeze or cough,
Anticipate some gas.
Cause even if you clench those cheeks
A fart is sure to pass.

The hairline starts receding
The sex life also wanes.
It's hard to rise on up from chairs
Without muscle aches and pains.

Bifocals now, not single lens
P's look like R's, and N's like M's.
Your hearing ebbs, your memory, too.
Your prostate, that's the bug-a-boo.

If turning fifty's not so nifty
In ten short years, you will be sixty.
Happy Birthday, Big Boy.

FOR FAMILY FRIEND FRANKIE

Frankie's birthday, we'll remember
To celebrate, we went to Denver.
Stowed our Harleys in a borrowed trailer
Got hit by a driver, drunk as a sailor.

400 bucks for the baseball game
Bought over Internet, they're to blame
Internet said the game start was at four
The game nearly over when we walked in the door.
Instead of seeing the game's beginning
We arrived in time for the 8th and 9th inning.

In one respect, our bad luck spared us.
The home run king was still Roger Maris.
What promised to be an exciting play,
Mark McGurie saved for another day.
So, on to dinner at the Denver Chop House
Hoped our motel wouldn't be a flop house.
Aspen was out, there was too much traffic
Besides, we were getting very psychopathic.

But here's to tell you what we're made of
Nothing will ever make us afraid of
Celebrating Frankie's birthday.
(Unless, of course, we have an earthquake.)
We laughed and had the greatest time.
Let's do it again when the birthday is mine.

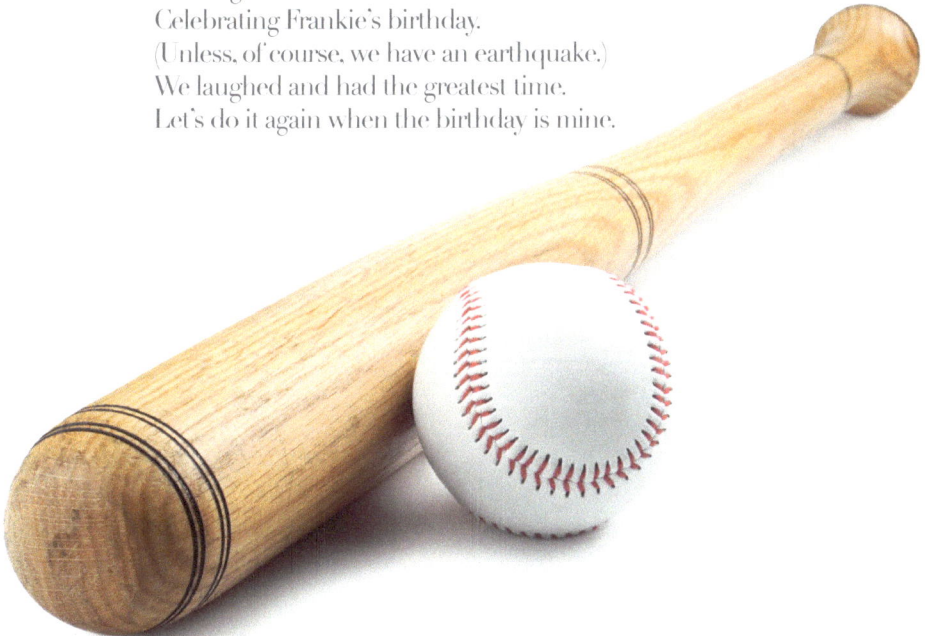

GAS, SASS AND OTHER INDIGNITIES

ODE TO A HUSBAND WHO FARTS IN BED

Pity The woman who wakes
as a bride
On the day after wedding
The dream boy beside
Her who's no longer
Single and doesn't recall
Lets go with a fart thats
The King of them all

Is this man beside her
the worst she has chose
Hand in hand through
the years, one hand hold-
ing her nose?
Of stopping this habit, he
makes no pretense
How do I stand it? I
fart in defense!

WRITTEN ON THE FRONT PORCH
RAPID CITY, AUGUST 13, 2004

I gave birth to four daughters who write
And make damn good money, in spite

Of the fact that I'm not paid
For the poems I have made.

Remember, don't ever forget
I'm the Hogue Family "Poet Laureate."

WRITTEN FOR NEW SON-IN-LAW TONY CALDARONE

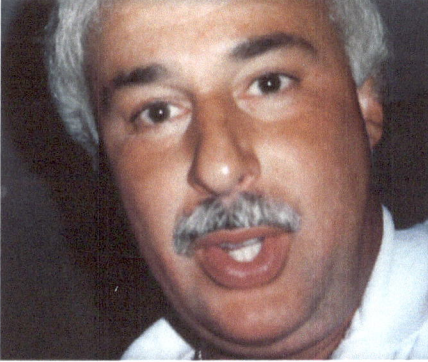

I understand you have a dog
And daily pick up shit.
I hear you do it gracefully
And don't complain a bit.

You also have a rabbit.
At least their crap is tiny.
But do they really shit all day?
Just plug his little hiney.

And then your fish - God, what a job.
Do you reach in and grab a blob?
Keep on working like the Dickens,
Then go to Linton and pick shit with the chickens!

I'll feed you well, I love to cook
And good food does abound.
But if you'd rather just eat out
There's restaurants all around.

And if you want to have some sex
My mattress doesn't squeak.
The bathroom's right next door
In case you have to take a leak.

If gas is just your problem
My window open wide.
If you check about the room,
There's scented sprays inside.

Please come and stay with us soon
I mean it from my heart.
Cause in our home you're welcome
To feed...and fuck...and fart.

POOR LITTLE PETEY

Poor little Pete
You're dead and gone.
From Berger's garage
To their back lawn.

You've left your buddies,
Chuck and Jesse.
The cage is now
One-third less messy.

You've flown inside
Those iron bars
And now you're up
Among the stars.

You've peeped and chirped,
Dropped turds galore
There's one less bird
To clean up for.

Oh, poor little Petey
I fear that he is dead.
I think his water bottle
Fell on his little head.

But when I filled the bottle
I blessed the contents of,
And now the holy water
Will send Pete up above.

Amen
Your grandmother, Pat,
unto whose care you
were entrusted.

UNITED WAY CHILI COOK-OFF

Step right up and eat our chili,
Savor every spoonful.
Beware the beans are potent, and
Will make you really tuneful.

To really have some fun with it
Let the aroma linger.
Then walk up to a friend of yours,
And have him pull your finger.

Your tummy growls, just like a bear
Let nothing spoil your day.
Gas attacks are natural
It's the United Way.

This chili that we serve you,
The best you'll ever eat.
Tomatoes, red as roses
Onions, oh, so sweet!

Before you pick that spoon up
We've just one thing to say.
The beans we used to make that soup
Will blow you to L.A.

Our chili makes you happy.
It also warms your heart.
And if you over-eat it
It's sure to make you fart.
This chili comes from Mexico

And this will come to pass.
Your gas won't come from Texaco
But surely from your ass.

So, eat a bowl, enjoy it
Our most delicious soup.
You'll notice two reactions,
You'll burp and then you'll poop.

We're doing this for charity
To help United Way.
We've made the tastiest chili
That you will eat today.

We used the best ingredients
And simmered it for hours.
You'll never taste another one
As soon as you've tried ours.

We're bound to win the top prize
I'll tell you from the start.
We'll also win a medal for
The way it makes you fart.

ODE TO DONNY SOFFER

This here's a love letter from Donny to Pat
inspired by the sweet sentiments of Don and
written by that oldest of all old song stylists... Ms.
Geri Atric

The song is performed by "The Genuine Jack
Daniels Band" with Boxcar Buster on spoon
and kettle top; Ms. Geri Atric on comb and Polly
Farton on the bottle and lead vocals.

It goes like this:

> Don't flush our love down the toilet.
> Patty don't flush it away
> Just promise to pee
> With no one but me
> And I'll promise never to stray.
>
> I'll put Tawny back on United
> And send her on home to L.A.
> Our love will go on
> If you don't flush the john
> Please don't flush our true love away.
>
> I miss seeing you in the kitchen
> The dining room and in the halls
> But when I'm alone
> I see you on the throne
> Oh, don't flush our true love away.

Donny and Patty attend the Hogue Family Reunion in the Black Hills, 1990

Precious Eddie

The greatest joy I've had in my life
Outside of my family, of course
Is the gift of my baby Maltese
From 4 of my kids was the source.

I gave him my dear father's name
His memories are all very sweet.
He, too, would have loved little Eddie
As Eddie swept us off our feet.

From a.m. to p.m. he's with us
And shares even our bed at night.
Of all of the dogs that I've seen
Eddie's the cutest in sight.

THE GAMBLER

It's getting near time for your drawing once more.
Again, I'm awaiting that knock on my door.
The flowers, champagne and the over-size checks
The limo outside adds to the effects.

I've waited for years just to win the big prize
At this point, I'd take one of any old size.
My patience is ebbing, my hopes getting low
I question that anyone wins all that dough.

I'm ever the finalist — on the inside
I'm always a bridesmaid, never the bride.
I'd like a new car, a Lincoln or Lexus.
But most of your winners I see come from Texas.

I live in Dakota — and Fargo's my home
Out where the Indians and buffalo roam.
There's never been anyone win from this state
If I were the first, it would really be great.

Being a finalist moved me to tears.
Once my father was one, he's been dead seven years.
Down through the years, I've bought more publications.
Hoping I'd win one of those nice vacations.

I've spent a small fortune
On all that you sell.
But if I don't win this time
You can all go to hell!

Mom and Mike hit the casino in Deadwood, SD.

ODE TO A SEARS POWER VACUUM

This morning while trying to clean up my home
I quit in disgust just to write you a poem.
I've suffered four years, gave my family much flack
Trying to cope with your Sears Power Vac.

I shopped for a vacuum, I wanted the best.
Consumer's Guide claimed that your Sears passed the test.
Your ads sounded great – I thought, "Gee, what a set-up"
Now I'm disillusioned and frankly, quite fed-up.

A Sears color console graces my den,
A Sears dryer dries all my clothes for my men.
Bread toasts in your toaster, our shoes are Sears leather
But your God-damn Sears vacuum won't pick up a feather.

I bought me the costliest model you had
And started my housework with venom.
It didn't take long for me to discover
I surely had purchased a lemon.

The plastic all cracked and the hoses did, too.
I'd take it back in for repair.
I'd pay a big bill, take it home, plug it in
It wouldn't pick up a dog's hair.

It bangs and it rattles, the gadgets are broken
No light, although sometimes the damn thing starts smoking.
For shags, pile or plush, it won't raise or lower.
I could use a toothbrush, it wouldn't be slower.

I'm frantically trying to clean up each room
And have to resort to my antique whisk broom
To clean up the dirt and the dust and the fuzz
That Sears vacuum ads say that it's machine does.

From normal housekeeping, my vacuum is battered.
My faith in Sears products has really been shattered.
My budget's too low to buy a replacement
But this one will soon join the junk in my basement.

And all this consumer has left Is her humor!

Always the Bridesmaid

Again I'm a finalist, just like last week.
Once more I will answer, your treasure I seek.
I don't care to order…there's naught that I need.
No things for the house, and nothing to read.

Again I am hoping for money or car.
I've prayed, called a psychic and wished on a star
That when round three ended and this was over
You'd call with good news…I'd be sitting in clover.

Please put Pat and Fargo on the map.
All of my family and buddies would clap
As the limo drives up with my oversized check
And I won't be giving you any more heck.
STILL NOT A WINNER!

Holy smokes – another deadline?
Hoped that I was now a headline.
Walking off with all that cash.
I'd start with throwing a big bash.

I'd treat my family, friends and 'geez
I'd even treat my enemies.
I'd pay my bills and buy a car
I'd take a trip and pretty far.

When winter comes in this cold land
I'd head for warmth and desert sand.
My fingers crossed and that's no joke
If I don't win, I'll have a stroke.

PUBLISHERS CLEARING HOUSE
pch.com
PORT WASHINGTON, NEW YORK 11050

Pay to the Order of **HEATHER BROWN**

$1,000,000.00 *Dollars*

0543:51025:011312:1600

AUTHORIZED SIGNATURE

To Mary and Tony on their Wedding Day

Today in Californ-i-a
Will be your glorious wedding day.
You'll all be in your finery
And marry at a winery.

Then off to Kath and Lee's to party
On turkey, ham and ala-cart-ee.
Tony, the happiest day of your life
Imelda out and a Norsk for your wife.

She'll love and treat you like a king
But I'll remind you of one small thing
Just so you know just where you're at
You're wife's a closet Democrat.
Mary, you're walking deep in clover
(His beautiful tan…is he tan all over?)
He's nice and loving and you will be, too
All day long, we'll be thinking of you.

All our love,
Mom and Dad
November 23, 1996

Mary, Tina, Tony and Michael Caldarone

On Teri's Marriage to Carl

I've waited all these years to have
A place to call my own
I share it with my love, Carl
But one spot I'm all alone.

It's in my yard, a special place
It's filled with plants and blooms
In open air, and breezy
Not stuffy like some rooms.

What I've loved the most of all
I noticed from the start
The best place I have ever been
To let a great big fart.

I fart among the peonies
And on those lovely roses.
Should others join me in my spot
They'd have to hold their noses.

I fart among the tulips
And on a buttercup
Sometimes I'm so excited
I have to mop it up.

I poop among the pansies
Pass gas on top of ferns
The more I let 'em have it
The more my butt hole burns.

I hope this will not stop
The growth of my flower garden.
For if it does, I'll have to ask
The good Lord for his pardon.

Teri and Carl Ciarfalio

49

PAT'S HAT

Here lies Pat's hat
It served her well
For four long years it looked like hell
Thru rain and snow and even sleet
It warmed her head - and sometimes feet!

HE STORY OF HARRY AND CHRISTY LYNN
COLLABORATION BY MOTHER & DAUGHTER

was a gorgeous summer day, the day
arry Lynn keeled over and died right
the middle of his beloved garden. His
ife, Christy, found him face up in the
rawberry patch, hands clutching his
eart, his dead eyes wide open, staring at
ut not seeing the sensational blue of the
idwestern August sky.

y parents took me to his funeral-it was my
st-and as I wandered through the crowd
fterward, I remembered listening to the
rown-ups as they said some really stupid
ings to each other, things like "Oh well, it
as probably his time to go," or "He should
ave taken it easy, he knew his heart was
d," or "Isn't it lovely that he died in the
rden? He would have wanted it that way."
dults were so dumb, I thought to myself.
hat on earth made them think Harry
anted to be dead?

hey just didn't know Harry the way I did.
fter all, I used to spend part of most every
mmer day in the garden with him and
e would talk about stuff. Harry would
l me about life and about how good it
as. We would talk about why the clouds
oked like floating elephants and why
od made it rain on picnics and why the
rden died every year. Harry would tell
e, "The garden doesn't really die. It just
es to sleep for a while; it needs the rest.
s like that with people. They don't really
e either. They go to sleep, too, but when
ey're rested enough, they wake up and
d they are living in a new, magical place."
I had to figure that Harry wasn't really
ead. He just fell asleep and was now living
the new, magical place, wherever that
s.

yway, the following summer came right
schedule and I went down to help

Christy with the garden. She had been so
sad all winter and now she seemed even
sadder. This would be her first summer in
the garden without Harry. So I helped her
like I used to help him, and together we
planted the corn, the tomatoes, the peas
that tasted so good right out of the pod and
the carrots that grew as long as rulers. We
tended to the strawberry vines that were
there on the spot where Harry died, in the
same place they had always been.

The garden grew magnificently, as it did
most every year, but this particular year the
strawberries wouldn't grow at all. Christy
thought this was strange, since strawberries
had always been Harry's best crop. They
would set up their fruit stand each summer
just to sell the strawberries, packed in those
cute little wooden baskets they bought at
Streyle's Hardware Store. Harry would
always have Christy make some of her
tangy, strawberry-rhubarb pies and jams
and jellies, and they would sell those, too.
But this year, with no berry crop, Christy
couldn't open the stand.
This event caused much speculation
among the locals. After all, the Lynn's
fruit stand was at the center of our lives
each summer. In fact, it was practically an
institution, like the fireworks stand out on
Highway 83. There were
theories galore
as to why the
strawberries
wouldn't grow.
Too cold, said
one neighbor.
Bugs, said
another. Mrs.
Fahlsing,
the local
seamstress
who thought

she was an expert on just about everything, said she thought there was a "nitrogen imbalance" in the soil. I thought there was an imbalance in Mrs. Fahlsing.

I had my own theory. I figured that because Harry was in the strawberry patch when he died, maybe he took those strawberry plants with him, and both Harry and the plants were awake and living in the new, magical place. It made perfect sense to me, but when I told that to my brother, he said I was nuts. I told Christy, too, and she just smiled sadly and stroked my hair as she gazed off into the sky. I swear I saw tears in her eyes. Anyway, the summer ended and the garden went to sleep for the winter, and everybody forgot about the strawberries and why they didn't grow.

It's been years since I've thought about any of this. I called my mother the other day to see what she remembered about that summer. We had a wonderful talk about Harry and Christy and how they filled our lives with so much love and joy. Mom couldn't remember why the strawberries wouldn't grow, but our conversation must have brought back some sweet old memories, because a couple of days later, she sent me this poem:

This is the poignant story
Of Christy and Harry Lynn
Behind their brick-walled garden
Is where this tale begins.

Harry loved to garden
Food and flowers are what he grew.
He spent his working hours there
Some sleeping hours, too.
He shared with us his bounty,
This green-thumbed gardener Harry.
His specialty and most prized crop
Was the beautiful strawberry.

The Lynns put up a food stand
"Fresh Berries" was the sign.
They canned, made pies and jellies
And they even made some wine.

Each year the plants produced more,
A big and sumptuous crop.
Then Harry got the bad news
That his poor heart might stop.

He wouldn't quit the garden
His wife was really shook.
And if he didn't hear her call
She'd search in every nook.
One day he didn't answer
So very scared she got,
She found him dead as a doornail
In his beloved strawberry plot.

The berries were ripe and juicy
And so his face was, too.
His body covered all the plants
The whole damn patch was goo.

The funeral was most moving
Poor Christy was distraught.
She couldn't face his garden
And the berries went to pot.

The next spring came and most plants
Rose up and grew so tall.
But Harry's prize strawberries
Wouldn't grow at all.

We can only guess at why
And Christy's had to face
That they went along with Harry
To, we hope, a better place.

So, while we miss his berries
That our stomachs use to fill,
I think that dear old Harry
Found his thrill on "Strawberry" hill.

Mom, Sammy, Patty and Dad

guess my mother-famous in our family for her "unusual" sense of humor, may have been
somewhat influenced by my version of what I think happened to those berries, but the
truth is we'll probably never know. I'm sure there is a perfectly logical explanation for why
the berries wouldn't grow, but I'm going to keep my childhood fantasy alive anyway, mainly
because it makes for such a wonderful memory.

Larry has been gong almost thirty years now, and, sadly, I've lost touch with Christy. But,
I never again look at a strawberry without being reminded of the Lynns and those special
ones I had with both of them back when I was a child.

STORY BY PATTY SOFFER
POEM BY PAT HOGUE
95

Buster and Willie

MOM'S
RECIPES

MOM'S CUSTARD

INGREDIENTS
12 slightly beaten eggs
1 cup sugar
1 tsp. salt
8 cups of scalded whole milk
4 tsp. vanilla

Add sugar to eggs and vanilla. Slowly stir in milk.
Pour into casseroles or custard cups. Sprinkle with
cinnamon. Bake in pans half full with hot water at
325° for 45 minutes or till a knife inserted in the
center comes out clean.

RECIPE FOR TWO
RHUBARB PIES
(what the hell is rhubarb, anyway?)

INGREDIENTS

1 1/2 cup flour
1/4 tsp. salt
1/2 cup oil
1/4 cup cold milk

Combine milk and oil in blender first. Then ad flour and salt and form
dough. Roll out and place in pie pans.
Combine 5 1/2 cups chopped rhubarb with 2 cups sugar.
Add 1 pint sour cream and 8 eggs. Pour into pie shells.
Sprinkle cinnamon on top.
Bake at 425° for 10 min., then 350° for 35 minutes.

BUSTER BARS

INGREDIENTS

1 pound package Hydrox cookies, crushed
1/2 cup butter
1/2 gallon vanilla ice cream
2 cups powdered sugar
1 can evaporated milk
1/2 cup butter
2/3 cup chocolate chips
1 tsp. vanilla
1 1/2 cups spanish peanuts

Mix cookie crumbs and butter. Press in a 9x13 pan. Put in fridge to cool. Spoon softened ice cream over crust. Put in freezer.

Combine sugar, milk, chips and butter in a saucepan. Boil 8 minutes, stirring. Add vanilla and cool. Sprinkle peanuts over ice cream and then pour cooled sauce over all.

Keep frozen. Keep Buster away.

BOILED HAM DINNER

INGREDIENTS

1 huge picnic ham
1 even bigger kettle

Cover ham with cold water. Put in bay leaf,
peppercorns and onions to taste. Bring to boil and simmer 1 hour. Cut up
potatoes, carrots, onions and celery, and put into pot. Lay cabbage wedges
and seasoned pepper on top. Cook 45 minutes more. Do not use salt in this
dish.

Will feed 8 very hungry Hogues, a Cornog or two and Jerome.

MOM'S SUGAR COOKIES

INGREDIENTS

2 cups margarine
2 cups Wesson oil
2 cups powdered sugar
2 cups granulated sugar
3 tsp. vanilla
2 tsp. lemon extract
4 eggs, beaten
2 tsp. salt
2 tsp. soda
2 tsp. cream of tartar
8 cups + 8 tbsp. of flour

Mix all ingredients except flour. Add flour bit
by bit and roll dough into small balls. Flatten
with bottom of a glass
that has been dipped
in (yes, you got it)
MORE SUGAR!
Bake at 375° for
10 minutes.

MOM'S FUDGE

INGREDIENTS
4 cups sugar
1 cup butter (2 sticks)
1 cup milk
2 1/2 tbsp. cocoa
1/2 cup syrup
1 pinch salt
Vanilla

Heat together, and do the "fudge test."
Add vanilla and beat in mixer till the shine
disappears. Pour in buttered dish. Eat.
Throw up. Repeat.

ICE BOX COOKIES

INGREDIENTS

2 cups brown sugar
2 cups white sugar
1 1/2 cups Crisco
Mix these together and cream.

Separate 3 eggs and beat whites till stiff. Add egg yolks and
beat. Fold into creamed mixture and beat. Add 1 1/2 tsp.
soda (in hot water) and 1 tsp. vanilla. Sift together 4 1/2
cups flour, 1 tsp. baking powder, 1 tsp cinnamon, 1 tsp. salt
and 1 tsp. baking powder. Stir into batter and add nuts.
Shape dough into long log-shaped rolls on waxed paper.
Refrigerate for an hour, then slice and put on cookie
sheets. Bake at 350° till golden brown.

Grandma Knudson always had a glass cookie jar filled with
these when we visited her in Pollock.

PETIT FOURS

INGREDIENTS
1 white cake mix
2/3 cup butter
1 pound confectioner's sugar
4 egg yolks
1 tbsp. vanilla
Ground salted peanuts

Prepare cake mix and cool. Cut into desired size pieces. Cream butter and add sugar and vanilla. Add 4 egg yolks and stir till creamy. Frost all 4 sides of cake and roll in crushed peanuts.

Messy, but worth it!

CHOCOLATE RUM PIE
(Makes 5 pies, 4 for Mike and 1 for everyone else)

INGREDIENTS
1 1/2 cups butter
7 cups powdered sugar
6 pkgs. chocolate (liquid packs)
3 tsp. vanilla
6 eggs

Mix in order. Beat in eggs, one at a time.
Chill in baked pie shells.

Vanilla pudding:
2 large packages vanilla instant pudding
    and 1 small one
2 cups thick cream
3 cups milk
1 tsp. rum flavoring

Mix and pour on top of chocolate mixture.
Top with whipped cream made with
powdered sugar, and shave chocolate on
top of pie.

500 DINNER ROLLS OR 250 CARAMEL ROLLS

Originally from the Dakota Farmer newspaper

INGREDIENTS

Soak 3 cakes of yeast in 3/4 cup warm water.
Boil together for 5 minutes:
   12 cups of water
   4 cups sugar
   3 cups Crisco
Cool to lukewarm.

Add 3 tbsp. salt
Stir in 12 beaten eggs
Stir in a small amount of flour
Then add yeast mixture and stir
Add enough flour to make a soft dough

Mix this up at around 6 a.m., and let rise till 12 p.m. Kneed down, and let rise.

Roll out dough, sprinkle with cinnamon and sugar, roll up and cut, then put into pans if making caramel rolls. Form dinner rolls, if making them. Let rise overnight.

In the morning, bake at 375°. For caramel rolls, mix up some cream and sugar and pour over rolls before putting them in the oven.

Then invite 250 friends over for breakfast.

DOUGH GLOBS AND THINGS

(If dough was really "dough" we'd have gone thru millions by now!)

INGREDIENTS

Start with 2 loaves of frozen bread dough. Place on cookie sheet, rub all over with Crisco, and let thaw in a warm spot.

If you want to make 'dough globs' slice off a piece, gently stretch and pop into a deep fat fryer till golden brown. Drain on paper towels. Serve with jelly, syrup, powdered sugar or whatever topping you like.

For "things," brown chopped meat, onions and seasonings, then add some sauerkraut. Drain this mixture in a colander and let cool.

Stretch out a piece of dough to cover your hand. Fill center with meat mixture and wrap the dough around it. Pinch the bottom to seal, and place on a cookie sheet, seam side down. Make a bunch, then bake for 10-15 minutes at 350° until golden brown. Place on rack to cool and brush butter on tops. Serve with ketchup for dipping.

Patricia Hogue

ABOUT THE AUTHORS

Some people are born talented beyond measure but are limited by opportunity, geography, money or timing. Many succumb to those limitations.

Patricia Hogue never allowed anything to limit her. Born of the Greatest Generation in a tiny South Dakota town, she maximized what she had been given and more than made up for in love, creativity, exuberance and wicked humor what she lacked.

The daughter of humble pioneer immigrants, Pat was sunny, funny and smart as hell. A college grad back when women weren't, she landed great friends and a teaching job in Grea Falls, Montana. But her greatest catch of all was Buster, whom she masterfully lured into her irresistible web and shared her life with for 60+ years.

Those were amazing years, with Pat prolifically producing successful children (with Buster's willing help), ridiculously good food, hilarious poems and stories, fun parties, holiday dinner for 40, a fresh-from-the oven haven for the neighbor kids, piano solos on the black keys and income thanks to Avon's door-to-door independence that enabled her to oversee a family lif so sweet that her six kids have found it impossible to replicate it in their own adult lives. Wh Because that particular sweetness requires Pat's constant presence. She is the anchor, the glu the maestro, the supporter, the taskmaster, the judge and jury, the voice in your head and hea and the sun, moon and stars.

But life moves on, and so has she. Today Pat is a sunny, funny nursing home resident in Nort Miami Beach, FL. Her memory has faded and her speech is challenged, but you know that like the peanut butter, she's in there somewhere, laughing and remembering. This book is h crowning achievement and before her decline into her brand of peaceful dementia, she han out copies to anyone and everyone who crossed her path. It brought joy to her and those wl read her words.

Well done, Pat, well done.

athy Berger

The second of six children, Kathy Berger grew up usually doing what "Mom Said." She was the daughter whose 30+ years of traditional married life and motherhood most closely mirrored her mom and dad's relationship. When that all fell apart, it was Mom's voice in her head that gave her the courage and sense of humor to hit the reinvention road, move to sunny Florida and use the next 10 years to become a successful businesswoman. Her mother's love of dogs must have also been another great inspiration, because Kathy now owns a retail and wholesale business dedicated to pets.

tty Soffer

Patty Soffer is her mother's daughter and then some. The product of a no-nonsense yet happy upbringing, she listened to her mother when she said, "Be sure to always have the means to take care of yourself." That one simple lesson drove Patty to a success as a NY model, high fashion boutique owner, co-owner of one of the South's top branding and design agencies and now, author of four (and counting) books. Her most recent title, *Partnership or Partnersh*t: You Decide*, pays homage to her mother's intolerance for bullsh*t. Perhaps this was her mom's greatest lesson.

For more information, go to ahumanfoundation.com

Hogue Family celebrates Buster's 70th Birthday

November 1993
Fargo, ND

Teri

Mary

Patty

Kathy

Pat

Eddie

Mike

Buster

Rollie